Easy Reading Edition
First published 1977

Macdonald Educational
Holywell House
Worship Street
London EC2 2EN

© Macdonald Educational
Limited 1977

Original edition
published 1975

Adapted by Ron Taylor
from the original text
by Solene Whybrow

Illustrators
Linda Broad
Ron Hayward Art Group
Debbie King
Pat Lenander
Laura Mason
Gill Platt
John Smith
Julie Stiles
Vanessa Woodward

Published in the United
States by Silver Burdett
Company, Morristown, N.J.
1979 Printing

Library of Congress
Catalog Card No. 78-56609
ISBN 0-382-06189-6

The Life of
Animals
with Shells

Macdonald Educational

The Life of Animals with Shells

There are many kinds
of animals with shells.
What is an animal's shell?
It is a hard cover
for the animal's body.

Crabs and tortoises
have hard covers
that we call shells.
But the biggest group
of animals with shells
is called the "mollusks."
Some kinds of mollusks
you may know very well,
for example, snails.
Many other kinds
of mollusks
live in the sea.

Most kinds of mollusks
live inside their shells.
But some cannot do so.
They have very small shells.
Some strange mollusks
have no shell at all.

This book describes
all kinds of mollusks
and the ways
in which they live.

At the end of the book
are some projects
for you to do.

Contents

What Are Mollusks?	8
Learning from Fossils	10
Looking Inside Mollusks	12
Feeding and Breathing	14
Mating	16
How Mollusks Grow Up	18
How Shells Are Made	20
Using Shells	22
Moving Around	24
Defense	26
Senses and Behavior	28
Where to Find Mollusks	30
Mollusks all over the World	32
Mollusks and Nature	34
Partners and Prey	36
Land Slugs and Sea Slugs	38
The Life of the Octopus	40
Strange Mollusks	42
Shell Art	44
Shell Collectors	46
Stories	48

Reference and Projects

Families	49
Explaining Some Words	50
Biggest, Smallest, Fastest, Rarest	52
How to Keep Water Snails	53
Shell Art for You	54
Making an Octopus	56
Making a Snail	57
Collecting	58
Keeping Your Shells	59
Index to Pictures and Text	60

These are mollusks

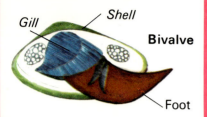

Bivalves have two-part shells. The parts are called "valves." In this picture one valve has been removed to show the animal's other parts.

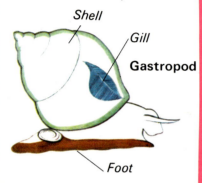

Gastropods, such as snails, have a one-part shell and creep about on a *foot*. Some breathe air with lungs, but most have gills.

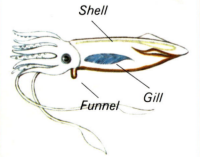

Squid, octopuses, and cuttlefish have big eyes and many arms. They do not have a *foot*.

Animals without backbones

You have a backbone.
A horse, a whale,
and a mouse
also have backbones.
Many big and small animals
have backbones.

But many, many animals
do not have a backbone.
Worms and crabs do not.
Jellyfish, fleas, and snails
do not.
Snails are mollusks.
Mollusks are animals
without backbones.

Mollusks' shells

A snail's shell
is like a house
built as one part.
Many mollusks
have one-part shells.

But many shells
that you find on beaches
are two-part shells.
Mussels have two-part
shells, so do oysters.
See the pictures
for other examples.

These are not mollusks

These four kinds of animals all have hard covers or shells, but **none** is a mollusk.

Barnacles are related to crabs, and sea urchins are related to starfish.
Brachiopods (brak-ee-o-pods) are related only to themselves.

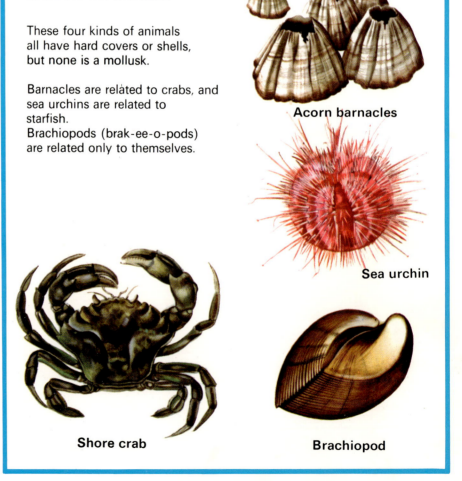

Acorn barnacles

Sea urchin

Shore crab

Brachiopod

Groups of Mollusks

There are five main groups of mollusks. Some groups have difficult names.

Bivalves

Mollusks with two-part shells are called "bivalves." This word means "two valves." In the pictures, the scallop, the razor shell, and the cockle are all bivalves.

Gastropods

Snails and slugs are called "gastropods," so are whelks, limpets, and cone shells (see the picture). Some gastropods have a one-part shell. Others have no shell at all.

Chitons

Chitons (ky-tons) have a shell made from eight separate pieces. These are held together by a kind of leather.

Scaphopods

Scaphopods (skafe-o-pods) have a long, tusk-like shell. They are also called "tusk shells."

Cephalopods

Cephalopods (keff-allo-pods) are the squid, octopuses, and the nautilus. Some have a shell, while others have no shell.

We know that mollusks have lived on earth for a very long time. We know this because we find their fossils.

Fossils can be millions of years old. Some mollusk fossils, such as ammonites, are very large.

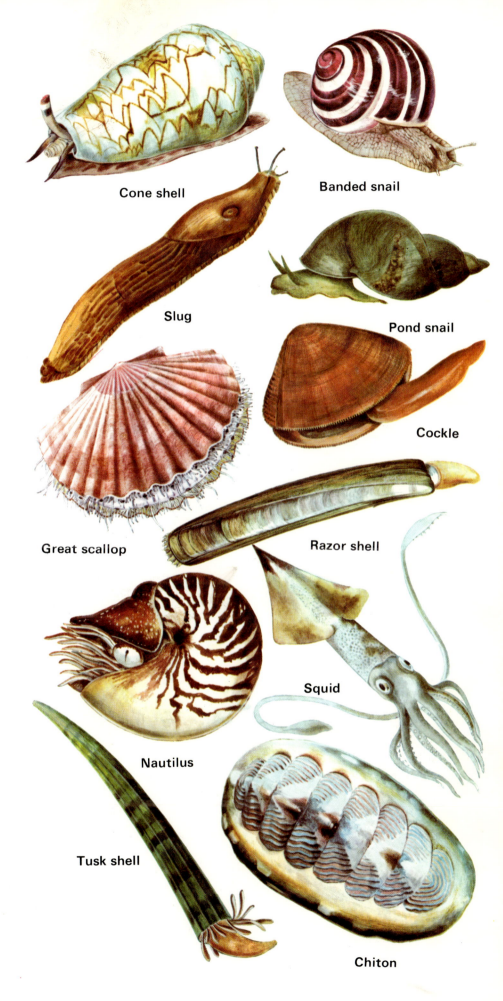

Cone shell

Banded snail

Slug

Pond snail

Cockle

Great scallop

Razor shell

Nautilus

Squid

Tusk shell

Chiton

Learning from Fossils

How fossil shells are formed

When a scallop dies, it falls to the floor of the sea. Its soft body is eaten by other animals. Its shell becomes buried in the sand or mud.

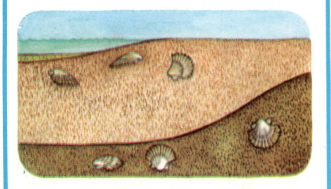

Sand and mud build up for thousands, or even millions, of years. This turns the sand or mud into rock.

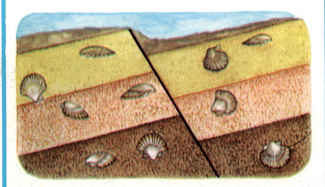

The shells, also, may turn into rock. They become fossils.
Then earthquakes may lift the rocks up, so we find fossils of shells in the land rocks.

Ammonite

Ammonites lived between 350 and 65 million years ago. They had an outside coiled shell with many chambers.

The monoplacophora were once thought to have become extinct 350 million years ago. In 1952, a living one called "Neopilina" was found off the coast of Peru. It resembles the fossil Pilina, which lived 400 million years ago.

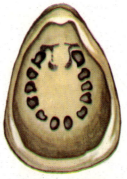

Pilina is a small fossil

Neopilina was found off the coast of Peru.

What are fossils?

Fossils are the remains
of plants and animals
that lived millions
of years ago.
We can find fossils
of sea animals
even in land rocks.
How we can do this
is shown by the pictures
on the opposite page.

Shell fossils

Only the hard parts of
an animal or plant
can become fossils.
Often the hard parts
have turned into rock.
How does this happen?

Water in the rock
dissolves away the hard
parts. This happens
very, very slowly.
As the hard parts
dissolve away, rock
begins to form.

The rock forms exactly
where the hard parts
were, so the fossil
looks exactly like
the hard parts once looked.

Some shell fossils are
found grouped together.
The shells were washed
onto a shore before
they became fossils.

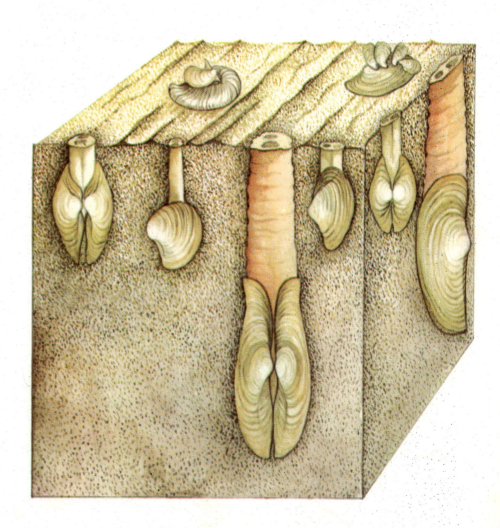

Some shell fossils are
found neatly arranged.
They show just how
the animals once lived.

11

Looking Inside Mollusks

Inside a snail

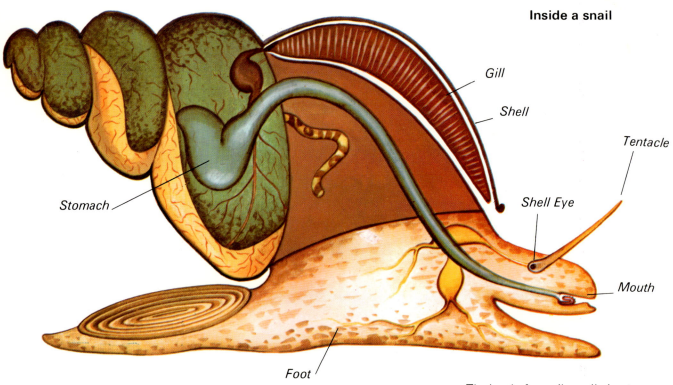

Stomach

Gill

Shell

Tentacle

Shell Eye

Mouth

Foot

The head of a snail usually has two eyes and tentacles. In the mantle cavity is the gill, which is used for breathing. On the top of the foot is the visceral mass which contains the stomach.

Inside a scallop

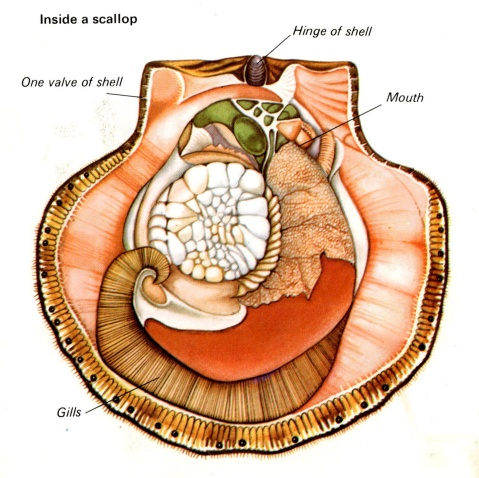

One valve of shell

Hinge of shell

Mouth

Gills

The name "bivalve" means having two shells or valves. Bivalves have no head and food is passed from the gills to the mouth.

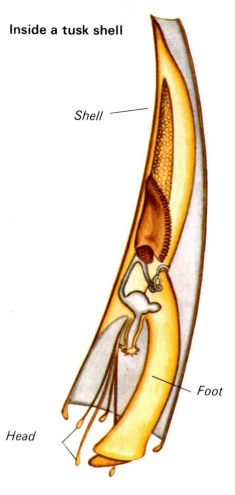

Shell

Foot

Head

Scaphopods, or tusk shells, are shaped like tubes and have openings at both ends. The shell is curved. Scaphopods do not have a head.

Mollusks

A mollusk has a soft body. It has no bones or other hard parts, except for its shell.

A mollusk protects itself by withdrawing into its shell. All of its soft parts are hidden inside its shell.

Mollusks' bodies

The pictures show various parts of mollusks' bodies. These parts include the soft, hidden parts and also the parts that can be withdrawn into the shell.

Mollusks' bodies are not at all like ours. Many mollusks do not have a head. The pictures on these pages show that neither the tusk shell nor the scallop has a head. The snail and the nautilus both have heads. They have eyes in their heads.

Inside a nautilus's mouth

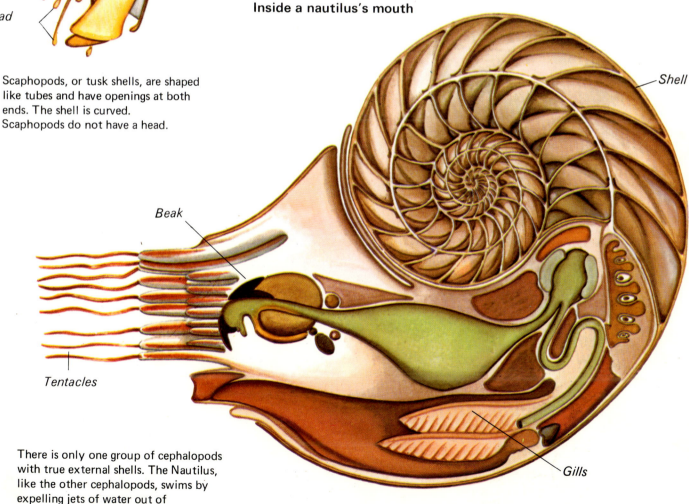

Shell

Beak

Tentacles

Gills

There is only one group of cephalopods with true external shells. The Nautilus, like the other cephalopods, swims by expelling jets of water out of its funnel. It breathes with jets.

Feeding and Breathing

Feeding

Some mollusks feed by *grazing*. They scrape bits off water plants and eat them. Mollusks, such as chitons, and also some snails, feed like this.

In their mouths they have a special scraper. It looks something like a tongue with teeth on it. It is called a "radula."

A whelk uses its radula to scrape small holes in the shells of other animals. Then it eats their soft parts. A squid also has a radula, but it chases and catches its prey.

Most bivalve mollusks feed quite differently. They filter tiny bits of food from the water and eat them.

Periwinkle

This periwinkle is feeding on seaweed. It uses its radula to scrape bits off.

Close-up of Periwinkle's radula

These mussels feed on tiny bits of food in the water. They draw the water in and *filter* out the food with their gills.

Mussels

Pond snail

River snail

Breathing

These mollusks breathe with lungs or gills. The land slug breathes with a lung. The sea slug breathes with gills. Both the snails live in water. How do you think they breathe? If you answer "by gills" you *could* be right. But some water snails breathe with lungs!

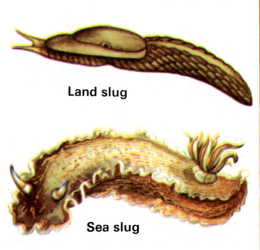

Land slug

Sea slug

Atlantic oyster drill

On each of these oysters is a little whelk. The whelks are boring holes in the oysters' shells. Then they will eat the soft parts of the oysters.

The cone shell in these pictures is catching a small fish. It puts out its sharp radula and sticks it into the fish. Poison from the radula stuns the fish. The cone shell pulls back the fish and eats it.

1

2

3

4

Mating

Roman snails

These snails are mating.
After mating, they will lay eggs.
The snails come together to mate.
Each snail is both a male
and a female!
Each snail gives the other sperms.
The sperms fertilize eggs
inside the snails' bodies.

These cuttlefish are mating.
The top one is a male.
He gives the female his sperms
through a special arm.
Both male and female have
bright striped shells.
These are their mating patterns.

Cuttlefish

An abalone (a-bal-oney) sheds its eggs, or sperms, into the water.

Abalone

Ways of mating

Mollusks have many ways of mating.
On the opposite page you can see how snails and cuttlefish mate.
These animals join together to mate.
But many mollusks do not join together to mate.
They simply shed their eggs or sperms into the water.
You can see above how the abalone sheds its eggs and sperms.

Fertilization

In all cases, the sperms *fertilize* the eggs. The eggs then *develop* into young animals.

Some mollusks are either male or female.
Most snails are both male and female.
Some mollusks begin as males, then turn into females.

Eggs of mollusks

Whelk eggs

Here are some mollusk eggs.
Some whelks lay long strings of eggs.
Other mollusks lay eggs in a kind of bottle.

When you go on vacation to the seashore do you ever find whelk eggs on the beach?

Sea slug eggs

Conch eggs

Nerite eggs

How Mollusks Grow Up

A cluster of squid's eggs

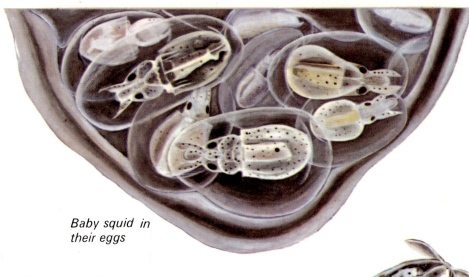

Baby squid in their eggs

How a squid hatches
A female squid lays her eggs
in a *cluster*. You can see a cluster
on the left.
Inside the cluster are lots of eggs.
Inside each egg is one little squid.
When the eggs hatch, the little squid
start to swim and grow.
They look like their parents.

A newly hatched squid

How an oyster grows up

Membrane

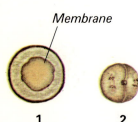

1	**2**	**3**

Cilia

4	**5**

Shell

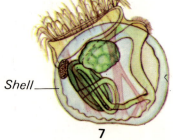

6	**7**

Oysters lay lots of tiny eggs.
You can see how one egg grows, or
develops, in pictures 1, 2, 3, and 4.

The oyster's egg develops into
a larva. The larva swims around by
waving little hairs called "cilia."

As the larva grows, it changes in
shape. Look at pictures 5, 6, 7, 8, and 9.

Hatching and growing

Mollusks lay eggs.
A land snail's egg
hatches into
a small snail.
But the eggs
of most water mollusks
hatch into larvae.

A mollusk larva
looks very different from
the grown-up mollusk.
See the pictures
of the larvae,
of a sea snail,
and an oyster.

Larvae are very small.
They swim around
by waving many
little hairs. These hairs
are called "cilia."

As the larvae grow,
they change in shape
until they become
the adult mollusks.

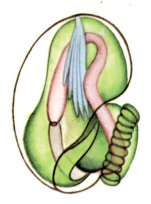
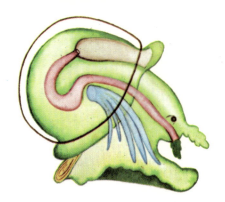

Twisting
On the left
is a sea snail larva.
On the right
is an adult sea snail.

You can see that
the body of the larva
has to twist in shape
as it grows up
to become the sea snail.

How old is a mollusk?
As a mollusk grows,
its shell also grows.
The shell gets bigger
by adding new rings of shell.
A mollusk expert
can tell a mollusk's age
from the number
of rings in its shell.

Great tellin

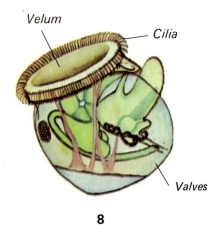

Velum

Cilia

Valves

8

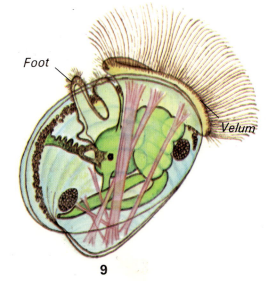

Foot

Velum

9

10

Now look at picture 10.
The larva has changed into an oyster.
After one year the oyster
has grown up.

How Shells Are Made

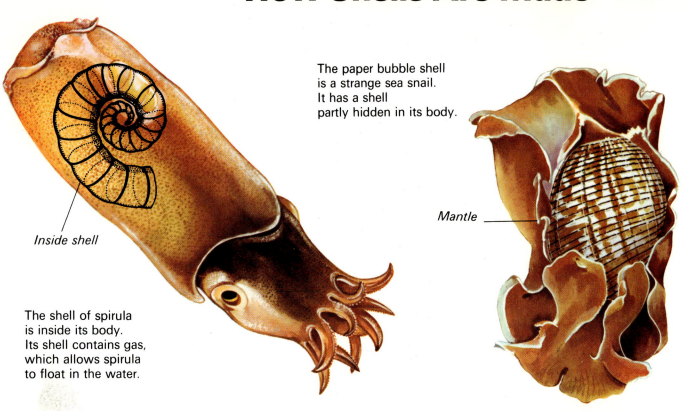

The paper bubble shell
is a strange sea snail.
It has a shell
partly hidden in its body.

Mantle

Inside shell

The shell of spirula
is inside its body.
Its shell contains gas,
which allows spirula
to float in the water.

Giant cockle

Sunrise tellin

**Strawberry
top shell**

Shell patterns

Mollusk shells
have many shapes,
colors, and patterns.

The pattern on
the sunrise tellin
is made by rings
of shells. These rings
show how old
the mollusk is.

Spotted cowrie

Venus comb

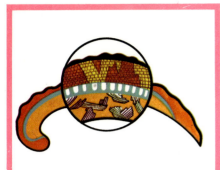

Shell layers

Shells are built from
four layers. Count them
in the picture.
In the bottom layer
you can see the
chalky crystals.

How shells are built

Mollusks make their shells.
They make them
from hard chalk.
They get the chalk
from seawater.

The chalk is *dissolved*
in the seawater.
Mollusks make
hard *crystals* of chalk
from this.
They build their shells
from these hard crystals.

If you look
inside an oyster shell
you can see a shiny
mother-of-pearl.
This is another
type of chalk
that mollusks make
from seawater.

Mollusks build
their shells slowly.
As they grow, their shells
become bigger
to hold their bodies.

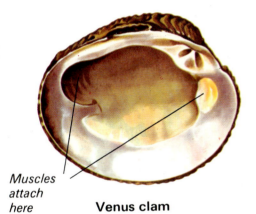

*Muscles
attach
here*

Venus clam

Living in shells

Bivalves, such as the Venus clam,
live inside two-part shells.
The two parts are held together
by strong muscles.
You can see where the muscles
attach to the shell.

Telescope shell

Nautilus

Other mollusks live inside
spiral shells. The nautilus lives only
in the last, largest chamber
of its spiral shell.
As the nautilus grows,
it adds bigger chambers to live in.

Using Shells

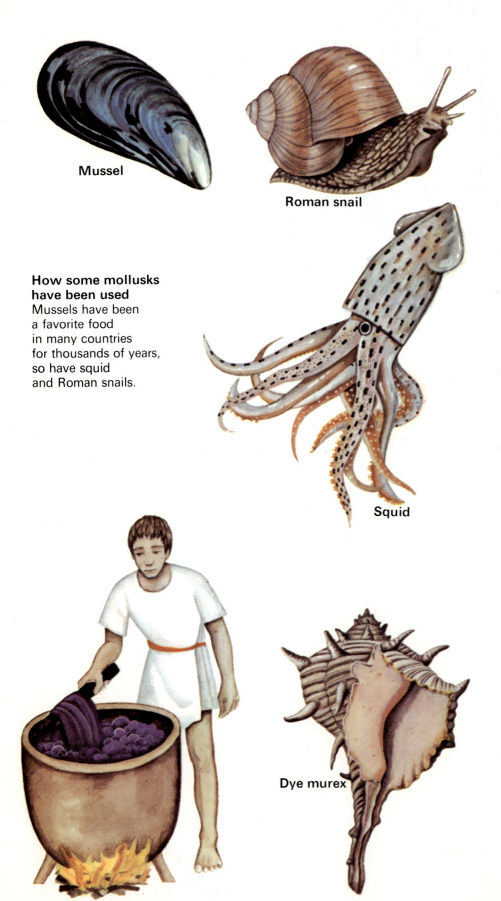

Mussel

Roman snail

Squid

Dye murex

How some mollusks have been used
Mussels have been a favorite food in many countries for thousands of years, so have squid and Roman snails.

Mollusks as food
Many people who have lived near the sea have liked eating seafood. Seafood includes crabs, prawns, and lobsters and, of course, many kinds of mollusks.

Today, most people like one or another type of mollusk food. Which kind is your favorite? Is it oysters, or clams, or perhaps, baby squid? Or do you just hate eating mollusk food?

Shell ornaments
For a very long time people have used shells as ornaments. Long ago, Stone Age people made bracelets from mollusk shells. You can still buy shell bracelets, necklaces, and buttons made from mother-of-pearl.

Long ago, rich people had their cloaks dyed a purple color. The dye was called "Tyrian purple." It came from the body of a mollusk called the "dye murex."

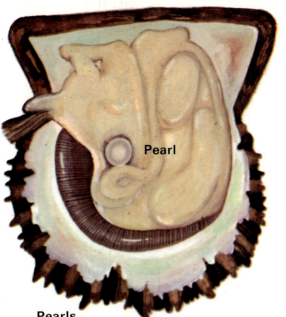

Diving for pearls

Pearls

The oyster makes its pearls from the same chalk that it uses for its shell. Divers swim down to collect oysters for their pearls.

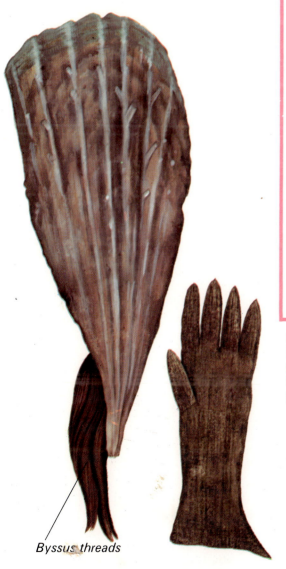

Byssus threads

Shell money

Mollusk shells have often been used as money. American Indians used clam shells and long strings of tusk shells. In the South Sea islands, cowrie shells were used as money.

Money cowrie

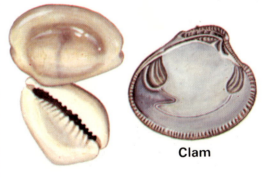

Clam

Tusk shells

Byssus threads

Pen shells tie themselves to rocks with byssus threads. Gloves can be woven from these byssus threads.

Wind chimes

These wind chimes are made from shells of a mollusk that lives in Japan.

Moving Around

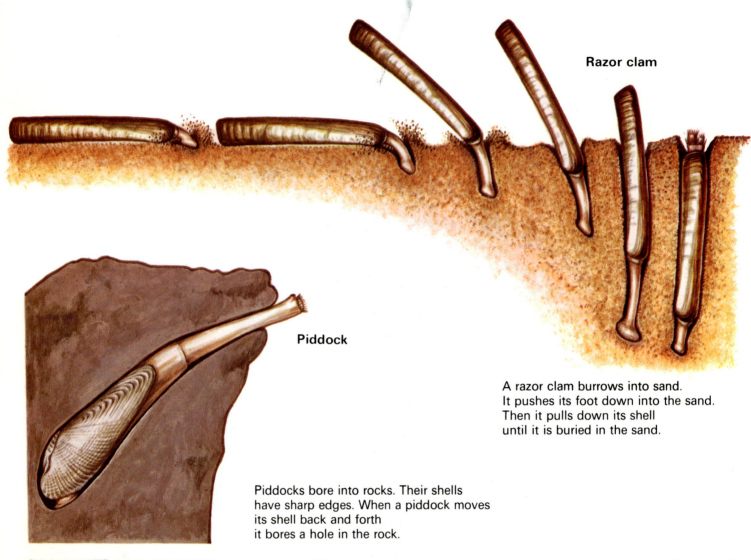

Razor clam

A razor clam burrows into sand.
It pushes its foot down into the sand.
Then it pulls down its shell
until it is buried in the sand.

Piddock

Piddocks bore into rocks. Their shells
have sharp edges. When a piddock moves
its shell back and forth
it bores a hole in the rock.

Starfish eat scallops. A starfish
creeps up on a scallop.

But the scallop makes a special
escape movement.

Slow and fast mollusks

Mollusks, such as snails,
whelks, and chitons
creep slowly
about on one foot.
Clams move about
even more slowly.
A clam puts out its foot
into the sand or mud.
Then it drags its body
slowly forward.

Mollusks, such as squid,
octopuses,
and cuttlefish
move much more quickly.
They squirt out
jets of water. This
pushes them
through the water
very quickly.

The pictures show
some other ways
in which mollusks move.

This snail is on a glass plate.
You see it from below. You
can see the wave movements
of its foot,
which move the snail along.

Violet sea snails
move around upside down.
They hang on to
a raft of bubbles.

It claps together the two valves
of its shell.

This blows water out and pushes
the scallop safely away.

Defense

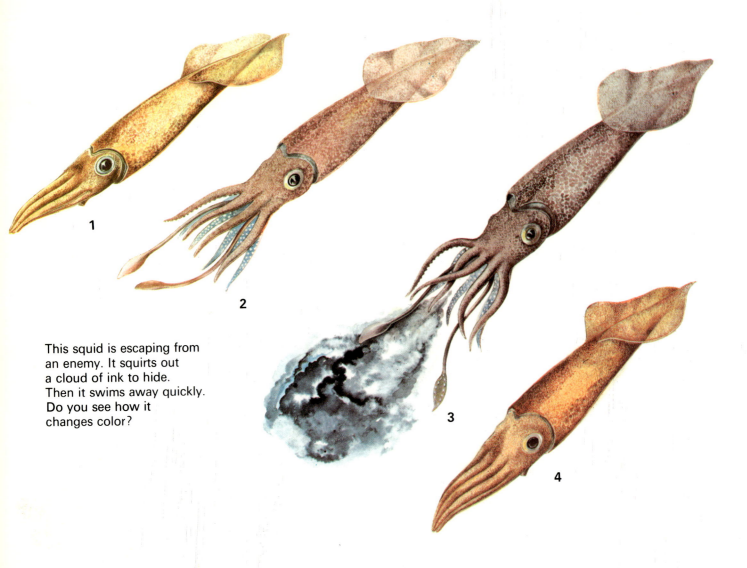

1

2

This squid is escaping from
an enemy. It squirts out
a cloud of ink to hide.
Then it swims away quickly.
Do you see how it
changes color?

3

4

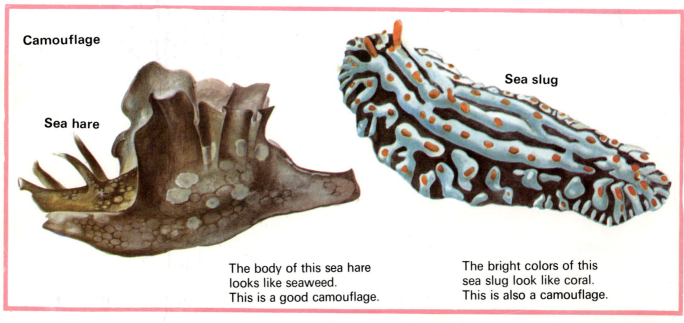

Camouflage

Sea hare

Sea slug

The body of this sea hare
looks like seaweed.
This is a good camouflage.

The bright colors of this
sea slug look like coral.
This is also a camouflage.

Clamping down

A limpet clamps down its shell into a groove that it makes in the rock.

Sea snail

Foot

Lid

Closing up

Many sea snails close off their shells with a sort of lid on the end of the foot.

Limpet

Shells protect mollusks

A mollusk's shell protects it from its enemies. Clams and limpets hide their soft bodies inside their thick shells. They are usually protected this way.

Colors and patterns

Some mollusks have only a small shell or no shell at all. These mollusks often use camouflage as a defense. Their bodies show colors and patterns that make them look just like their surroundings. Then their enemies cannot see them. Other mollusks have bright colors that warn enemies: "Keep away—I am poisonous!"

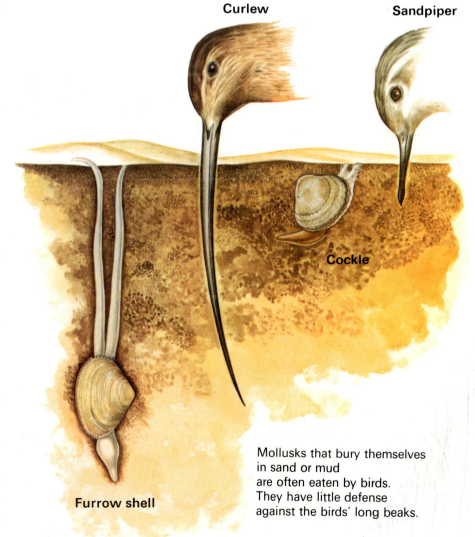

Curlew

Sandpiper

Cockle

Furrow shell

Mollusks that bury themselves in sand or mud are often eaten by birds. They have little defense against the birds' long beaks.

Senses and Behavior

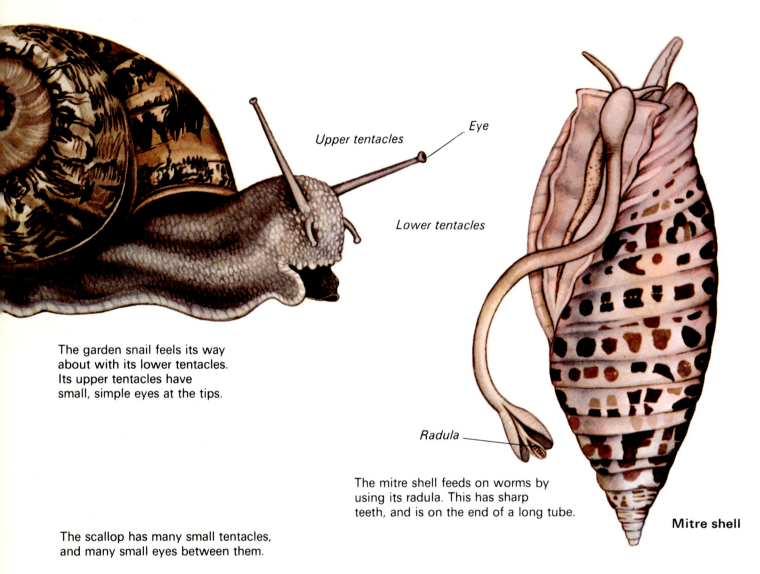

Upper tentacles

Eye

Lower tentacles

The garden snail feels its way about with its lower tentacles. Its upper tentacles have small, simple eyes at the tips.

Radula

The mitre shell feeds on worms by using its radula. This has sharp teeth, and is on the end of a long tube.

Mitre shell

The scallop has many small tentacles, and many small eyes between them.

Scallop

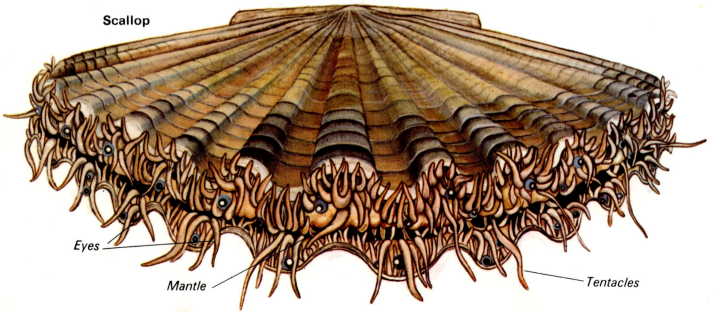

Eyes

Mantle

Tentacles

Touch and smell

Like ourselves, mollusks
have a sense of smell.
Usually, they find
their food by its odor.

Mollusks also have
a sense of touch.
A cuttlefish feels things
with the suckers on
its arms.
A snail feels things
with small tentacles
on its head.

Sight

A snail has small eyes
on its tentacles.
A scallop has many
small eyes.
Their eyes see only
lights, shadows,
and movements.

Octopuses, squid,
and cuttlefish
have large eyes.
Their vision
is as good as ours.

Deep sea diving

A cuttlefish can dive deep down
into the sea. Its shell helps it
to withstand the great pressures
of the sea water. The shell
is inside its body. It is called
a "cuttlebone."

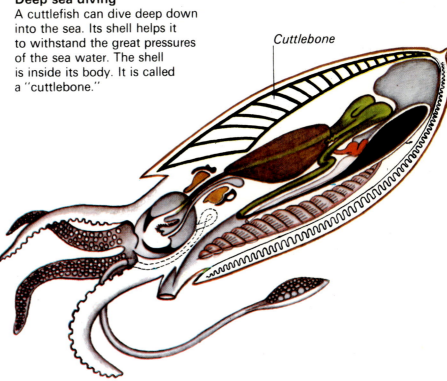

Cuttlebone

Winter sleep

When winter comes, snails
creep underground
or under dead leaves.
They seal off the opening
in their shells.
Then they sleep until spring.

A harp shell catches crabs in a strange way.
It drops off a piece of its body.
A crab comes along to eat this.
Then the harp shell catches the crab
and eats it!

29

Where to Find Mollusks

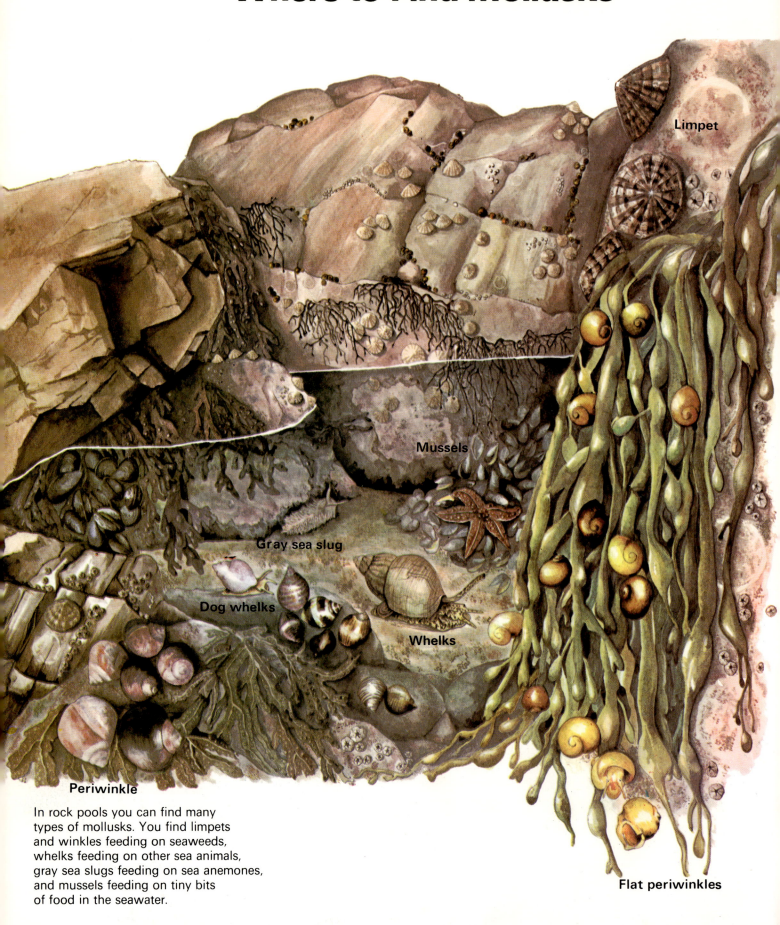

Limpet

Mussels

Gray sea slug

Dog whelks

Whelks

Periwinkle

Flat periwinkles

In rock pools you can find many
types of mollusks. You find limpets
and winkles feeding on seaweeds,
whelks feeding on other sea animals,
gray sea slugs feeding on sea anemones,
and mussels feeding on tiny bits
of food in the seawater.

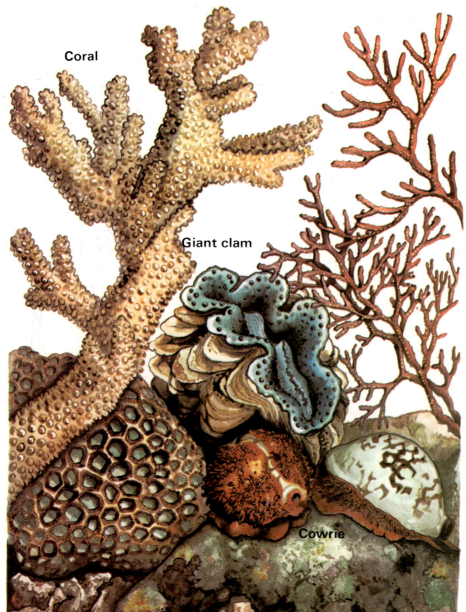

Coral

Giant clam

Cowrie

Sea and land

Mollusks live in most
parts of the world.
Most live in the sea,
while others live on land,
or in rivers and lakes.
You can find
many different types
of mollusks
on the seashore.
Some live buried
in the sand.
These include cockles
and razor shells.
Some live on rocks,
such as limpets
and winkles.
Others, such as piddocks,
 bore deep into rocks.

Oysters and other bivalves
live on the sea floor
in shallow waters.
Many squid live deep
down in the sea where
there is no light.
They light their own way
with special light organs.

In warm seas, mollusks,
such as clams and cowries,
make their homes under corals.
Other mollusks bore deep into
corals to make their homes.

Tree snail

This snail lives only
in the very tops of tall trees
on a South Sea island.

31

Mollusks all over the World

On ocean waves
This snail floats in the sea, upside down on its raft of bubbles.

On the seashore
Large conch sea snails, as well as other mollusks, live on sandy seashores.

In shallow seas
Oysters, clams, and scallops are mollusks that live on the floors of shallow seas.

In deep seas
This squid is swimming in shallow water. But squids can also live miles deep in the oceans.

Studying mollusks
If you want to know a lot about mollusks, then you must look for them and study the ways in which they live.

A very good place to look for mollusks is the seashore. Look in places where the sea tides cover up the beach at least once each day. Take a spade and dig up cockles and razor shells that live buried in the sand or mud.

If you live in the tropics, then perhaps you can swim down to a coral reef to study mollusks. Anyone can find snails in meadows and ponds. If you live in the tropics, look also in the trees.

On ships and in docks
Mollusks, such as limpets, cling to ships' hulls. Piddocks bore into concrete in docks. Other mollusks bore deep into wooden piers.

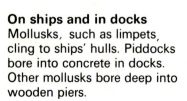

Tusk shell

Gaper

New England nassa

Shells of cool seas

Mollusk shells have a wide variety of colors and designs. Most large shells in the northern hemisphere are dull white in color. The shells are often thicker than those in the tropics. This may help to protect the mollusk from freezing.

American oyster

Lightning whelk

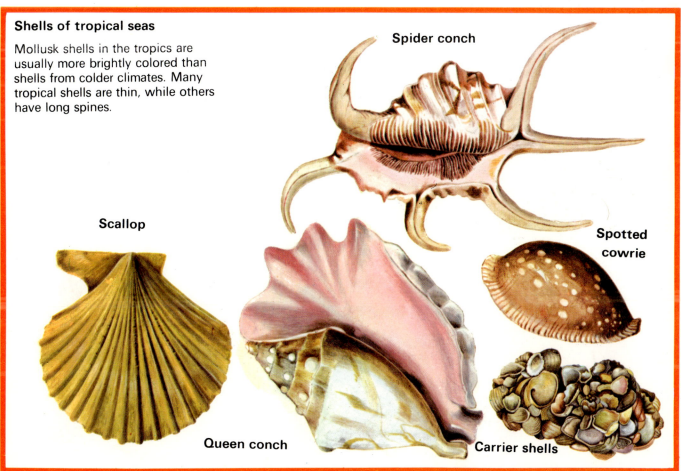

Shells of tropical seas

Mollusk shells in the tropics are usually more brightly colored than shells from colder climates. Many tropical shells are thin, while others have long spines.

Spider conch

Scallop

Spotted cowrie

Queen conch

Carrier shells

Mollusks and Nature

On this beach, thousands of mollusks have been killed by oil spilled from a ship.

The role of mollusks

Each animal and plant has a special place in nature. Each one lives in a special way, important to nature. Mollusks, like other animals, have their own places in nature.

Some mollusks are like the sheep of the sea. They graze on seaweeds and on tiny floating life in the sea. These mollusks are eaten by larger animals, which are eaten by still larger animals. This is called a "food chain." You can see some food chains in the pictures opposite.

Some diseases are spread by snails, as shown in the picture on this page. Often, many mollusks die because of *pollution* caused by man.

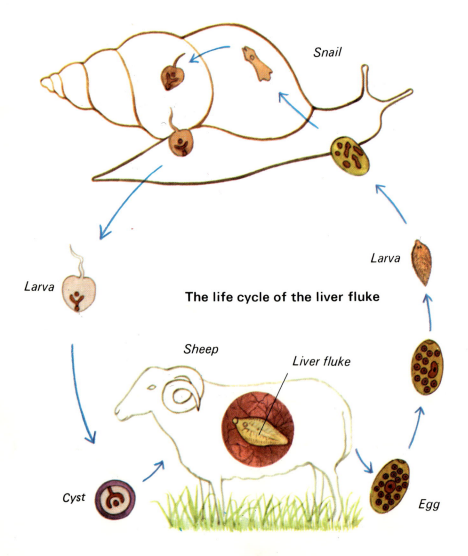

Snail

The life cycle of the liver fluke

Larva

Larva

Sheep

Liver fluke

Egg

Cyst

The sheep suffers from a disease caused by a liver fluke. The snail spreads this disease, because it carries a larva of the liver fluke inside its body. The eggs of the liver fluke drop on the grass with the sheep's droppings. When the sheep eats the grass, it catches this disease.

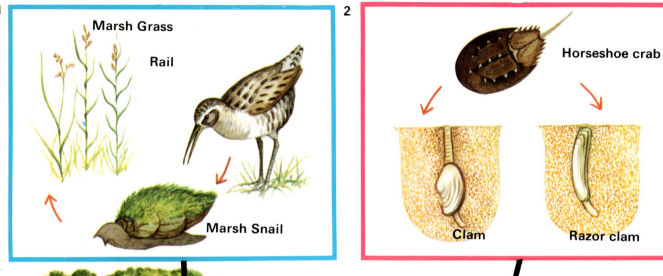

1

Marsh Grass

Rail

Marsh Snail

2

Horseshoe crab

Clam

Razor clam

3

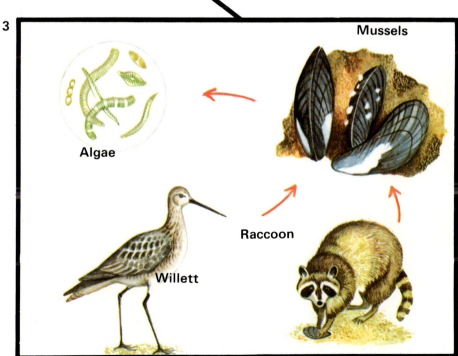

Mussels

Algae

Raccoon

Willett

Food chains on a salt marsh
See picture 1. This shows a bird
that feeds on a snail, which feeds
on marsh grass. This is called a
"food chain."

See picture 2. This shows two mollusks
that are eaten by a horseshoe crab.
This is a short food chain.

See picture 3. This shows a raccoon
and a bird that both feed on mussels,
which feed on tiny plants called "algae."
This is a longer food chain.

Partners and Prey

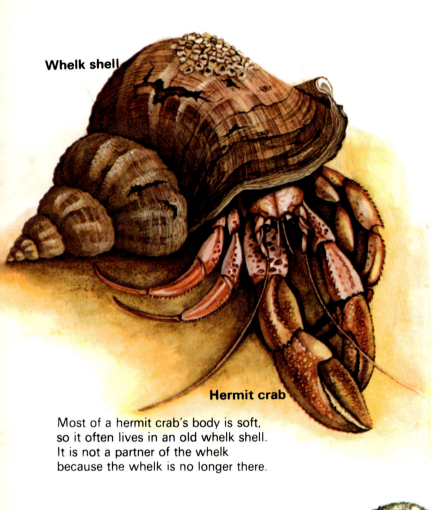

Whelk shell

Hermit crab

Most of a hermit crab's body is soft, so it often lives in an old whelk shell. It is not a partner of the whelk because the whelk is no longer there.

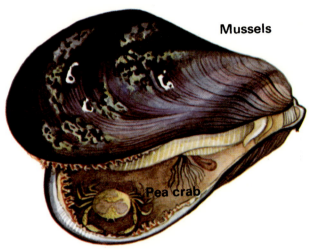

Mussels

Pea crab

The little pea crab lives inside the mussel's shell. The two animals share their food. The crab is protected by the mussel. They are partners.

The mantle of the giant clam is a bright blue color. This is caused by millions of tiny blue algae that live in the mantle. The clam and the algae are very close partners.

Giant clam

Algae

Partners

Some animals live together with other animals. They are partners. Mollusk partners include the mussel on the opposite page. This mussel is the partner of a crab.

Another mollusk partner is the giant conch snail. This allows a small fish to live inside its shell. The conch snail and the small fish share their food.

Prey

Often animals that live together are *not* partners. On this page are three pictures of mollusks that *prey* on other animals.

Cyphoma Snails

Sea fan

The sea fan looks like a plant, but it is an animal. The sea snails feed on the sea fan.

The gray sea slug is a mollusk that feeds on sea anemones. So the anemone is the *prey* of the sea slug.

The blue sea slug lives together with a jellyfish called "velella." They are not partners, because the sea slug eats the velella's tentacles. It gets its blue color from them.

Sea anemone

Gray sea slug

Velella

Blue sea slug

Land Slugs and Sea Slugs

Land slugs

Pictures on the opposite page show some land slugs. Slugs are like snails, but they have very small shells, or no shells at all. Some slugs have small shells inside their bodies.

Sea slugs

Sea slugs are related to land slugs, but they look very different. Most sea slugs have very bright colors. They are among the most beautiful of sea animals. Sea slugs breathe either through gills or through their skin.

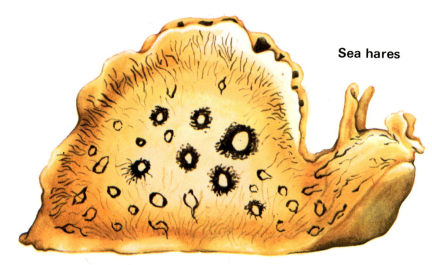

Sea hares

Spotted sea hare

Pictures on these two pages show the three kinds of sea slugs. Look at the picture above. This shows a sea hare. A sea hare is a large sea slug that has a small shell inside its body. Look at the pictures below. They show some dorid sea slugs. These are mostly small. Look at the lower picture on the opposite page, which shows some eolid sea slugs. These are also small animals.

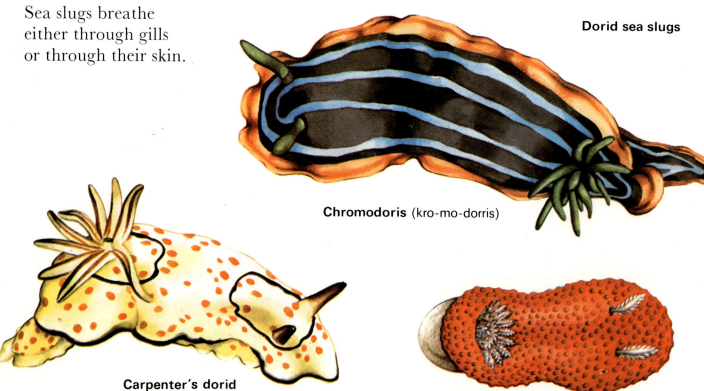

Dorid sea slugs

Chromodoris (kro-mo-dorris)

Carpenter's dorid

Red dorid

Land slugs

Land slugs breathe
with a lung.
On two of these slugs,
you can see the opening
to the lung.
The other land slug
has a small shell
on its body.

Shelled slug

Round backed slug

Keeled slug

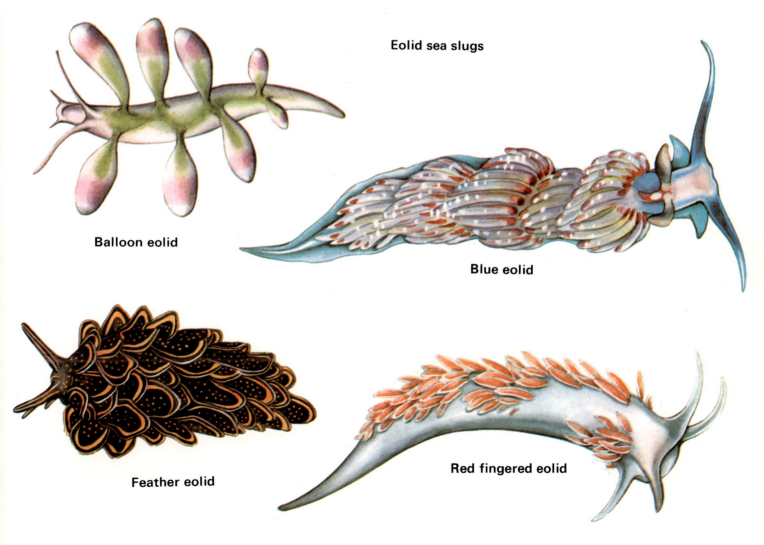

Eolid sea slugs

Balloon eolid

Blue eolid

Feather eolid

Red fingered eolid

The Life of the Octopus

The clever octopus

Octopuses are mollusks without shells. They have bigger brains than most other mollusks. Their eyes are large like our own eyes.

An octopus is a shy animal. It hides in a hole in the rock. When a crab comes by, the octopus rushes out and grabs the crab and eats it.

Eight arms

Octopuses and their relatives all have eight arms. These are covered with suckers. An octopus picks up and holds things with its suckers.

An octopus swims by squirting out a jet of water. This pushes it along. An octopus defends itself by squirting out a cloud of ink.

Egg clusters

The argonaut is a relative
of the octopus. She has a
very thin shell, like a paper
bag. She carries her eggs in it.
The male argonaut is only 1/20th
her size, about as big as your thumb!

The umbrella octopus has large webs
between some of its arms. It uses
its webs to catch fish and
jellyfish.

This female octopus has laid her eggs
and hung them up in clusters in a cave.
She has just eaten a crab. You can see
the crab's claws.

Strange Mollusks

This strange mollusk lives
in mud on the deep sea floor.

Worm shells are strange
mollusks related to snails.
Many of their shells
get stuck together like this.

Strange creatures

All mollusks are strange
animals. No mollusk is
like any other kind
of land or sea animal.
One mollusk on this
page looks a little
like a worm. But its
body, inside, is not at
all like a worm's body.

Some mollusks
are even stranger
than others.
The sea butterflies
on the opposite page
are related to snails,
though they do not look
like them at all.

Mollusks are a
varied group of animals.
They include octopuses,
snails, shipworms,
and clams. None of these
mollusks look like
any of the others.

The carrier shell is a sea snail
that sticks other shells
all over its own shell
as a disguise from its enemies.

This little green mollusk
is related to snails,
but it has a shell
made in two parts
like a clam's.

The watering pot shell
is a bivalve mollusk,
like a clam or a mussel,
but its two-part shell
is very small.

Ship worms are also
bivalve mollusks. Their
shell is very small and sharp.
They use the shell
to bore deeply into wood.
Ship worms cause a lot of damage
to wooden boats and piers.

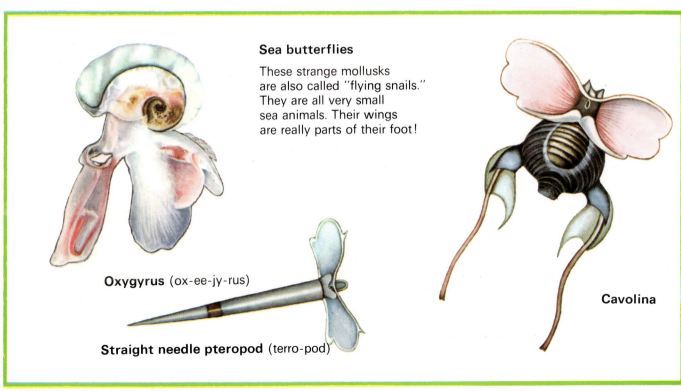

Sea butterflies

These strange mollusks
are also called "flying snails."
They are all very small
sea animals. Their wings
are really parts of their foot!

Oxygyrus (ox-ee-jy-rus)

Straight needle pteropod (terro-pod)

Cavolina

Shell Art

This death mask is made
from a skull. Its eyes
are made from cowrie shells.
The death mask was made long ago
in the city of Jericho.

Stone Age people made
shell necklaces like this.

The octopus is a design
on this pottery flask.
The flask was made in Crete
about 3,300 years ago.

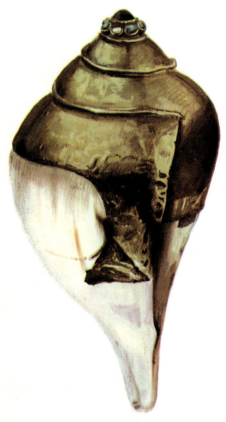

This chank shell comes from India.
It is used in a Hindu temple,
and is covered with gold and jewels.

Aztec shell trumpet

A conch shell trumpet
was blown to tell the
Aztec people
that their king was coming.

A carving on a shell, like this carving of a head, is called a "cameo." This cameo is carved on a helmut shell.

These happy flowers and the vase that they stand in are all made from colored shells.

Shell ornaments

Do you own a shell necklace or bracelet? Does anyone in your family own one of these? If so, then you know that shells are often used as ornaments. Mother-of-pearl, from inner parts of shells, is used to make jewelry. It is also used to make pearly patterns on furniture.

Shell grottoes

In the 1700s and the 1800s, rich people used shells to decorate rooms in their big houses. They called these rooms "shell grottoes." You can see a shell grotto on this page.

This shell grotto is at the house of the Duchess of Richmond at Goodwood Park, England.

Shell Collectors

A shell collector chases a scallop for its shell.

Shell collections

Do you like to collect shells? You can find many types of shells on seaside beaches. Common types include whelk shells, mussel shells, scallop shells, and cockle shells. Can you name two other common types of shells?

If you are very lucky you might find a large conch shell. Some shells are very rare. Collectors will pay lots of money for very rare shells.

Shell collectors collect shells for fun and also for study. The study of shells is called "conchology" (conch-ollo-jee).

Common nerite shells

Thorny oyster

Trumpet shell

Glory-of-the-sea cone

Slit shell

Eyed cowrie

Some rare shells

Sundial shell

A rare murex

Imperial volute

47

Stories

Some stories tell of "man-eating" giant clams. But no clam could ever eat a person! Possibly, a giant clam could hold a diver under water for a while.

An old Welsh legend tells of a saint who protected people from snakes by turning the snakes into stone. But now we know that these "snakes" are really fossil mollusks!

Many stories have been told of giant sea monsters. Such monsters really exist! Giant squid can grow up to 18 meters (60 ft) in length!

Families

The family tree

In this book you can read about many types of mollusks. Some have very long names, which were given to them by scientists. The names were given so that each mollusk can be separated from other mollusks. This is how scientists classify mollusks.

See the family tree on this page. It shows how mollusks are related. For example, clams are closely related to scallops, but are not as closely related to snails. Try to fill in the spaces: Whelks are closely related to .... but not as closely related to ....

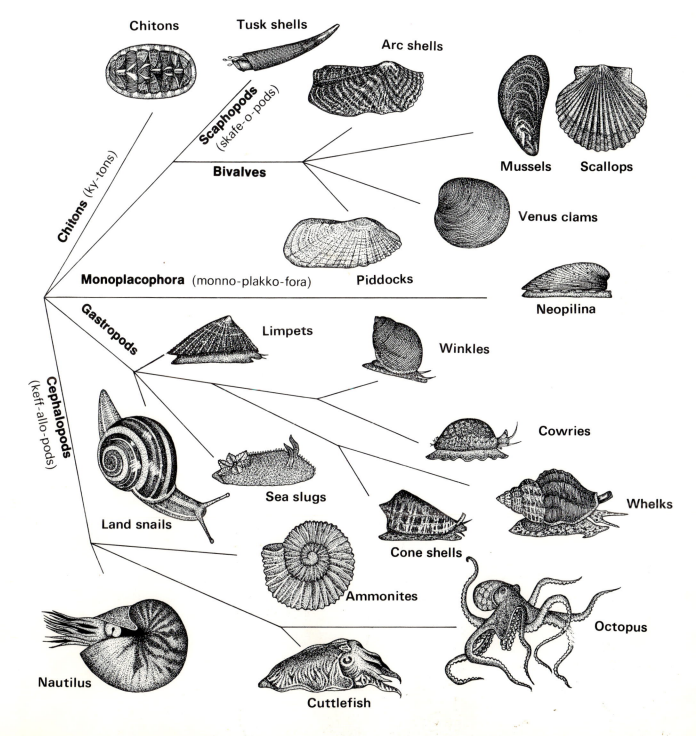

Chitons

Tusk shells

Arc shells

Scaphopods (skafe-o-pods)

Chitons (ky-tons)

Bivalves

Mussels   Scallops

Venus clams

Monoplacophora (monno-plakko-fora)

Piddocks

Neopilina

Gastropods

Limpets

Winkles

Cephalopods (keff-allo-pods)

Cowries

Sea slugs

Whelks

Land snails

Cone shells

Ammonites

Octopus

Nautilus

Cuttlefish

Explaining Some Words

Algae
Very, very small plants.
Some algae have only one
cell. Algae live in water
and in damp soil.

Ammonites
Mollusk fossils with flat,
coiled shells.

Arms
Squid, octopuses, and
cuttlefish all with long
arms on their heads.

Beaks
Found on some types of mollusks.
Squid, octopuses, and
cuttlefish
all bite their prey
with a beak.

Bivalves
Mollusks that live
inside two-part shells.
The two parts are hinged
together like the covers
of a book.

Brachiopods
(brak-ee-o-pods)
Animals without backbones
that have two-part shells.
Brachiopods are *not*
mollusks. Many millions of
years ago, thousands of
types of brachiopods lived,
but most of these have since
died out.

Byssus
Threads that some mollusks
use to bind themselves to rocks.
Mussels have a byssus.

Camouflage
(kam-eh-flaj)
Many mollusks have colors
and patterns that look
very much like their surroundings.
This makes it difficult for
their enemies to see them.

Cephalopod
(keff-allo-pod)
The group name for squid,
octopuses, cuttlefish,
and nautilus.

Chitons
(ky-tons)
Mollusks that have shells
made of eight separate pieces.

Cilia
(silliee-ah)
Tiny hairs that some
mollusks use to wave small
bits of food into their mouths.

Conchology
(conch-ollo-jee)
The study of shells.

Crystals
Hard solids with regular
shapes. Look at sugar and
salt. They both are made
up of crystals.

Cuttlebone
The shell of a cuttlefish.
It is inside the cuttlefish's
body.

Dissolving
Sugar *dissolves* in tea.
Seawater has many salts
dissolved in it.

Fertilize
A sperm fertilizes an egg.
You started your life as
a fertilized egg inside
your mother's body.

Filtering
Have you ever poured tea
through a filter or strainer so
that tea leaves did not
get into the cup? That is filtering.

Filter feeding
Some mollusks, such as
mussels, feed by filtering
out small bits of food
from the water.

Flukes
These are small, flat worms
that can cause serious
illnesses to humans and
animals.

Food chain
When a small animal or
plant is eaten by a larger
animal, which is eaten by
a still larger animal, and
so on, this process is called
a "food chain."

Foot
A mollusk's foot is usually
a large muscle. Snails
walk on their feet. An
octopus does not have a foot.

Gastropods
(gas-tro-pods)
Snails and their relatives
have a one-part shell.

Gills
Many mollusks breathe
under water with gills.

Grazers
Mollusks that feed by
scraping bits off leaves
and seaweeds with their
radula. (See Radula.)

Hibernate
(hy-ber-nate)
Animals hibernate when
they go into a winter sleep.

Larva
The young of many types
of mollusks.
A larva does not look
like its parents.

Larvae
(lar-vee)
The plural
of larva.

Lung
Many land mollusks, such as
snails and slugs, have a lung
to breathe air.

Marine
A marine animal is one that
lives in the sea.

Monoplacophora
(mono-plakko-fora)
The oldest of all types
of mollusks. Most kinds
are fossils, but one kind
called "neopilina" still
lives.

Mucus trail
(mew-kuss)
The slimy,
shiny trail that a slug or
snail leaves behind it.
Mucus protects a mollusk's
foot from rough ground.

Parasite
A parasite lives in, or on,
the body of an animal or
plant and does it harm.
Flukes are parasites (see
page 34).

Pearls
Mollusks, such as oysters,
make pearls from a sort of
chalk that they get from
seawater. (They also make
their shells from chalk.)

Pollution
Spoiling air, water, or soil
with unpleasant or harmful
gases, liquids, or other
substances.

Predator
An animal that attacks and
eats smaller animals.

Prey
An animal that is attacked
and eaten by a larger animal.

Radula
A "tongue with teeth"
that many mollusks have
for breaking up their food
into small pieces. Snails
wear away bits of leaves
with their radula. Squid
and octopuses first bite their
prey with their beak (see
Beaks) before breaking it
up with their radula.
Mussels, and other filter
feeders (see Filter feeding),
have no radula.

Scaphopods
(skafe-o-pods)
A group of mollusks that
include tusk shells (see picture on
page 9). Scaphopods have
a long, slightly curved
shell open at both ends.
They have no head or gills.

Shellfish
A common name that we give to
crabs, shrimps, prawns, and
many mollusks that we eat.
Of course, not one of these
animals is really a fish!

Sperms
A male animal makes sperms
in his body. He gives
sperms to a female to
fertilize her eggs. (See
Fertilize.)

Tentacles
A snail has tentacles on its
head. A scallop has tentacles
along the opening of its
shell. (See page 28 for
pictures.) A nautilus has
tentacles on its arms (see
page 13). Mollusks use their
tentacles mainly for feeling
and tasting.

Tropical seas
Seas in which the temperature
of the water is usually about
23°C.

Valves
The names of the two parts of
a bivalve mollusk's shell. (See
Bivalves.)

Biggest, Smallest, Fastest, Rarest

The biggest octopus
Octopuses are never so big as some of
the stories told about them! The biggest
ever caught measured more than 7 meters (21 ft)
from tip to tip of its arms. But its body
weighed only 50 kilograms (100 lbs).

The oldest mollusk
Neopilina (nee-o-pill-ina) is a
little mollusk first found in 1952.
(See picture on page 10.) It lives
more than three kilometers (1 3/4 mi) down in
the Pacific Ocean. All its relatives died out
more than 320 million years ago.

The largest shell
The Giant Clam lives on coral reefs. It has
a shell up to 110 centimeters (3 ft) wide and
70 centimeters (1 1/2 ft) broad. It weighs up to
one fourth of a ton. (See pictures on pages 36 and 48.)

The rarest shell
The white-tooth cowrie shell has been found
only three times in the deepest parts of
the oceans. Collectors sometimes pay about $2000.00
(£1,000) for a shell.

The longest life
Some mollusks can live to be very old.
Some mussels that live in fresh water can
live to be 100 years old. A giant clam
lives to be about 30 years old.

Fastest and slowest snails
The world's fastest snails can speed up to
50 meters (100 ft) per hour. But some snails can
only reach speeds of 60 centimeters (1 1/2 ft) per
hour. If one of these snails kept going,
without resting at all, it would travel
one kilometer (3300 ft) in about 11 weeks.

Deadly cone shells
Two types of cone shells kill their prey
with a deadly poison. (See pictures
on pages 9 and 16.)
Both deadly cone shells live in
tropical seas.

The largest pearl
The largest pearl ever found was in a giant
clam. This pearl was 23 centimeters (9 1/2 ins)
across and weighed 7 kilograms (14 lbs). It is
called the Pearl of Lao-Tse.

The smallest octopus
Most kinds of octopuses are not very large
animals. But one octopus from Ceylon
measures only 5 centimeters (2 ins) from the head
to tip of its arms.

The most deadly octopus
The small blue ringed octopus, from tropical
seas, has a deadly poison. It uses its
poison to kill its prey. The poison is
so strong that it can kill a person in
a few minutes.

The smallest mollusk
Octopuses have the best brains of any mollusk.
In fact, octopuses are the smartest of
all animals without backbones. Because they
are smart, scientists study how they behave,
and teach them tricks.

The largest snail
The largest snail lives in Africa. Its name is
"achatina." It can grow up to 30 centimeters (1 ft)
long, with a shell 20 centimeters (8 ins) long.

The largest mollusk
The largest mollusk is the Giant Squid. (See its
picture on page 48.) It is also the largest of all
animals without backbones. It can grow up to 17
meters (45 ft) long from the tips of its arms to the
tip of its "tail."
Giant squids live in deep seas. They are attacked
and eaten by sperm whales.

Largest shell collection
A man named Hugh Cuming collected nearly 100,000
shells. Most of these shells are located in the British
Museum in London.

Left-hand shells
If you look at the way that a snail's shell coils,
you will see that it coils to the right or
clockwise. Now look at the way a whelk shell
coils. It also coils clockwise. But very rarely will a
shell coil the other way, to the left,
or counterclockwise. You can see a picture of a
left-coiling shell on page 44. This is a sacred
chank shell.

How to Keep Water Snails

Studying snails

Water snails are the easiest mollusks to keep and study. You can keep snails quite easily in a glass water tank or an aquarium.

Fill your tank with water from a pond or river. Make a "floor" in the tank with some gravel and sand or mud. Then lay a few stones in the tank. These are useful to hold down some water weeds. Weeds will keep the water fresh and will provide food for the snails.

You can buy pond weeds from some pet shops, or collect your own weeds from a local pond. Keep your snail tank in a light, airy place, but *not* in bright sunlight, because it will get too warm.

See the pictures of the different kinds of snails that you can keep. Also, you can keep fresh water mussels in the tank. You can study how the snails move and feed, and also how they breed.

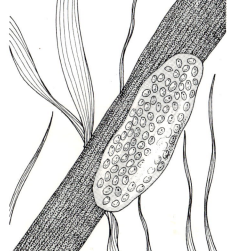

Egg mass of pond snail

Ear pond snail

White ram's horn snail

Great ram's horn snail

Great pond snail

Dwarf pond snail

Moss bladder snail

Shell Art for You

Shell box

Shell brooch

Shell flowers

Shell lamp base

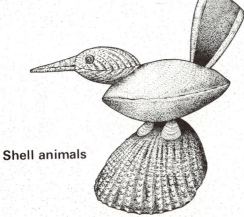

Shell animals

Shell Gifts

If you have a lot of shells, use them to make any of the "shell art" gifts on this page. To glue shells to bottles or boxes, use a thick layer of paste. Stick the shells well down in the paste. To make shell flowers, stick one shell to another with strong glue.

When you have finished gluing down your shells, let the glue or paste to dry. Then paint your "shell art" with clear varnish. This will make the shells shine.

Soft toy snail

Soft toy octopus

Making an Octopus

What you need
Gray felt. Scraps of white and black felt. Stuffing. Glue.

The pattern
Draw the octopus pattern on paper as shown. You can draw the squares bigger, if you like, to make a bigger octopus.

Cutting out
Put the pattern on your gray felt. Draw around the pattern with a soft pencil. Then cut out the "arms" shape and the 4 "body" shapes.

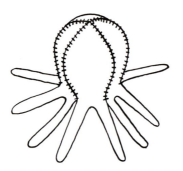

Sewing
Sew together the 4 "body" shapes as shown. Fill the body with stuffing. Then put glue on the middle of the "arms" shape, and stick it on to the body.

Cut round pieces of white and black felt for the eyes. Stick these on to the body with glue (see octopus on page 55).

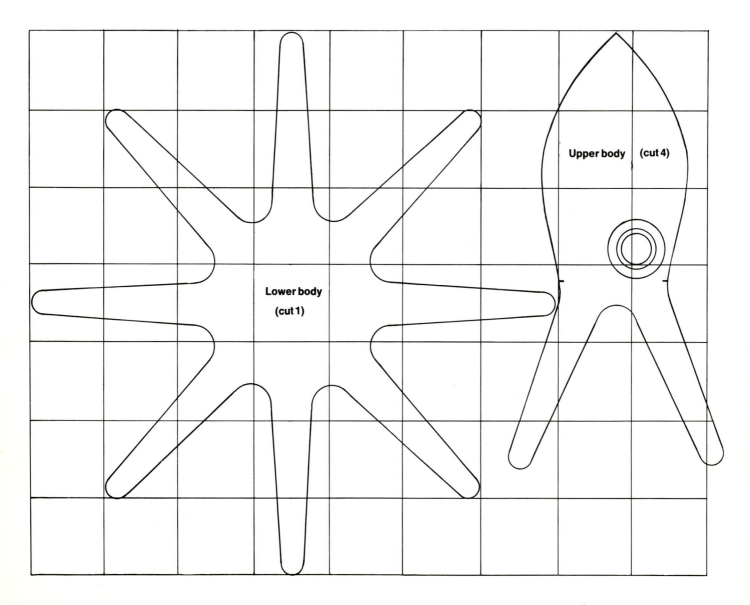

Lower body

(cut 1)

Upper body   (cut 4)

Making a Snail

What you need
Felt (choose your own colors). A scrap of black felt. Colored thread. Stuffing.

The pattern
Draw the snail pattern as shown (you can draw it bigger if you like). Put the pattern on your felt, and draw around it with a soft pencil.

Cutting out
Cut out 2 "snail" shapes, one "front face" shape and one "foot" shape.

Sewing
Sew each of the snail shapes to a side of the "front face" shape. Then sew in the "foot" shape leaving a gap for the stuffing. Put in the stuffing, then stitch the gap. Embroider the spiral, and stick on two black bits of felt for eyes as shown on page 55.

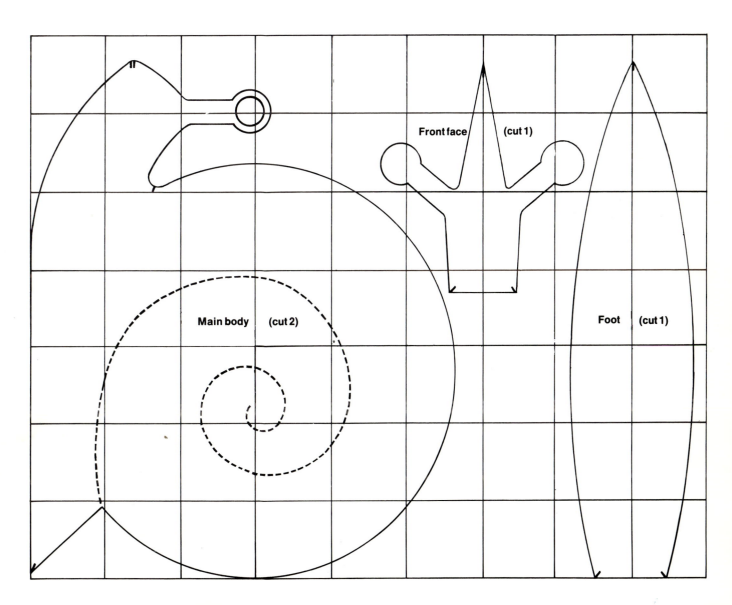

Front face (cut 1)

Main body (cut 2)

Foot (cut 1)

Collecting

Observing sea animals

While you are "hunting," be as quiet as you can. If you splash around noisily, most animals in a rock pool will hide. You will never even see them. When you make a "find," you can write down where you made it. Then you will know where to look the next time. Do not forget to write a label for each of your "finds," so that you know what is in each collecting tube.

Sea animals are difficult to keep. Many die soon after you collect them. Put the animals back in the ocean after you have examined them.

Mollusk shells

You can learn a lot about mollusks by collecting their shells. Anyone can pick up shells on a beach. But to make a good collection, you will need to search in other places as well. You will need to search in rock pools and other wet places. You will need clothes that are waterproof, and sea boots.

You will need some of the things shown in the pictures. Keep all of the smaller things dry inside a waterproof bag. Then you will be ready to begin searching, even in damp, cold places.

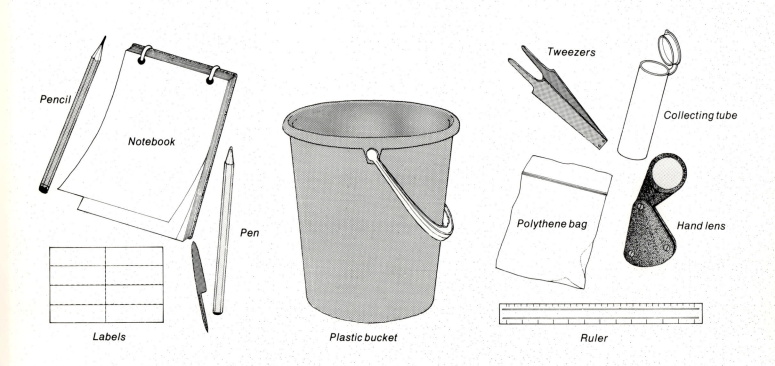

Pencil

Notebook

Pen

Labels

Plastic bucket

Tweezers

Collecting tube

Polythene bag

Hand lens

Ruler

Keeping Your Shells

Collecting empty shells

If you collect a lot of shells, you will need somewhere to keep them. You will need a shell cabinet like the one in this picture.

Each type of shell can be put away in its own cabinet tray. A tray can hold several small shells of the same kind. You can make each tray from a matchbox.

But before you put your shells away, you must clean them. First, soak them in hot water. Then scrub them clean with a toothbrush. Be careful with the thinner shells. Dry your shells on a soft towel and lay them on cotton wool in their trays.

Labeling shells

Put a label on each tray in your shell cabinet. Write on the label the name of the shell. In the picture, you can see a tray labeled "Murex," because it contains a murex shell.

Next, write down all details of the shell on an index card. Write the name of the shell, and where and when you found it. Also, do not forget to write down which tray the shell is kept in. Keep all your index cards in a card index file. Then you can look up the details of any shell.

You can also keep a book, called a Shell Catalog (kat-a-log) in which you also put down all details of your shells.

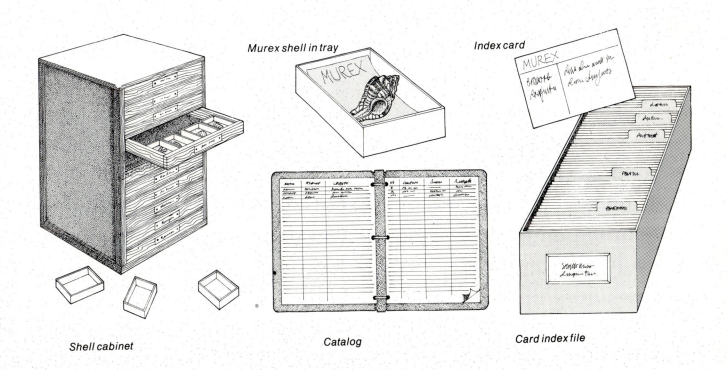

Murex shell in tray

Index card

Shell cabinet

Catalog

Card index file

Index to Pictures and Text

The numbers in **bold type** show where the pictures are.

Abalone, **17**
Age of mollusks, 19
Algae, **35**, 36, 50
Ammonites, **9**, **49**, 50
Anatomy of mollusks, **12–13**
Animals without backbones, 8
Aquarium, **53**
Arc shell, **49**
Argonaut, **41**
Arms of mollusks, 50

Banded snail, **9**
Barnacles, **8**
Beaks of mollusks, 50
Bivalves, **8**, 9, **12**, **49**, 50
Brachiopods, **8**, 50
Breathing of mollusks, 14–15
Bubble raft, **25**
Burrowing, **24**
Byssus threads, **23**, 50

Cameo (shell), **45**
Camouflage, **27**, 50
Carrier shells, **33**, **42**
Cephalopods, **8**, 9, **20**, **22**, **26**, **32**, **40–41**, **49**, 50
Chank shell, **44**
Chitons, **9**, **49**, 50
Cilia, **19**, 50
Clams, **21**, **23**, **31**, **36**, **48**, **49**
Cockles, **20**, **27**
Collecting shells, **46**, **58**
Collector's kit, **58**, **59**
Comb shell, **20**
Conch shells, **32**, **44**
Conch shell eggs, **17**
Conchology, 50
Cone shells, **9**, **47**, **49**
Coral, **31**
Cowrie shells, **20**, **23**, **31**, **33**, **47**, **49**
Crabs, **8**, **36**
Crystals, **21**, 50
Curlew, **27**
Cuttlebone, **29**
Cuttlefish, **8**, **16**, **49**

Defenses of mollusks, 26–27
Difficult words, 50–51

Eggs of mollusks, **17**, **40**, **53**

Facts and figures, 52
Family tree of mollusks, **49**
Feeding of mollusks, 14–15
Fluke, **34**, 50
Flying snails, **43**
Food chains, 34, **35**, 50
Foot, of snail, **25**, 50
Fossil mollusks, **9**, 10, **49**
Furrow shell, **27**

Gaper shell, **33**
Gastropods, **8**, **9**, **12**, **14**, **49**, 50
Gills, 14–15, 50
Grazers, 50
Groups of mollusks, 9, **49**

Harp shell, **29**
Hatching of mollusks, 18–19
Helmet shell, **45**
Hermit crab, **36**
Hibernation, **29**, 50
Hinge of bivalve shell, **13**
Horseshoe crab, **35**

Ink of mollusks, **26**, 38

Jellyfish, **37**
Jewelry, shell, **44**

Larvae, **18–19**, 34, 50
Limpets, **27**, **30**, **49**
Liver fluke, **34**
Lung, 15, 50

Marine, 50
Marsh snail, **35**
Mating of mollusks, **16–17**
Mitre shell, **28**
Mollusk groups, **49**
Mollusk partners, **37**
Mollusks' prey, **37**, **40**
Money, shell, **23**
Monoplacophora, 8, **10**, **49**, 51
Moss bladder snail, **53**
Mother-of-pearl, 22, 44
Movement of mollusks, 24–25
Mucus trail, 50
Mussels, **14**, **22**, **30**, **35**, **36**, **49**
Murex shells, **22**, **44**, **59**

Nassa shell, **33**
Nautilus, **9**, **21**, **49**
Nautilus' organs, **13**
Neopilina, **10**, **49**
Nerite eggs, **17**
Nerite shells, **17**, **46**

Octopus, **40**, **41**, **49**
Octopus eggs, **40**
Oysters, **18–19**, **33**, **47**

Parasite, **34**, 51
Pearl divers, **23**
Pearls, **23**
Pen shell, **23**
Periwinkles, **30**
Piddocks, 24, **49**
Places where mollusks live, 30, 32
Pollution, **34**, 51
Pond snails, **9**, **15**, **53**
Predator, 50
Prey, 50
Projects for you, 53–59

Radula, **12**, **14**, **28**, 51
Rail (bird), **35**
Raccoon, **35**
Ram's horn snail, **53**
Rare shells, **47**
Razor shells or razor clams, **9**, 24
River snails, **15**
Rock pool, **30**
Roman snail, **22**

Salt marsh, **35**
Sandpiper, **37**
Scallops, **9**, **28**, **33**, **49**
Scallop's organs, **12**
Scaphopods, **9**, **49**, 51
Sea anemone, **37**
Sea butterflies, **43**
Sea fan, **37**
Sea hare, **26**, **38**
Sea slugs, **26**, **30**, **37**, **38**, **39**, **49**
Sea slug eggs, **17**
Sea snails, **27**, **37**
Sea urchin, **8**
Senses of mollusks, 28–29
Shellfish, 51
Shells, 7, 20–21
Shell art, **44**
Shell grotto, **44**
Shell ornaments, **22**, **49**, **54**
Shipworms, **43**
Slugs, **9**, **15**, **39**
Snails, **8**, **9**, **15**, **22**, **31**, **35**, **49**, **53**
Snails' eggs, **53**
Snails' organs, **12**, **28**
Snails' tentacles, **28**
Sperms, 51
Soft toy snail, **55**
Soft toy octopus, **55**

Spiral shells, **21**
Spirula, **20**
Squid, **9**, **22**, **26**, **48**
Squid's eggs, **18**
Starfish, **24**
Strange mollusks, **42–43**
Suckers, 29, **40**

Telescope shell, **21**
Tellin shell, **20**
Tentacles, **28**, 51
Top shell, **20**
Tree snail, **31**
Tusk shells, **9**, **23**, **33**, **49**
Tusk shell organs, **13**
Tyrian purple, **22**

Umbrella octopus, **41**

Valves (of bivalve shells), 51

Water snails, to keep, **53**
Watering pot shell, **43**
Whelks, **30**, **33**, **36**, **49**
Whelk eggs, **17**
Willett (bird), **35**
Winkles, **30**, **49**
Winter sleep, **29**
Worm shell, **42**